The two Great Gray Owls landed silently in a pine tree in the North Woods. Apollo, named after the god of sun, spoke to his partner, Venus, named after the goddess of love, "We made it back here to find a good nesting spot."

After checking several trees, they chose a spruce tree.

Venus commented quietly, "This nest isn't the best, but not the worst."

The nest was next to a clearing, a stream, a meadow, and hidden from above by large branches. The owls settled into the nest.

It wasn't long before Venus announced there were two eggs in the nest. Apollo was to stand guard and cover the nest if Venus was to leave.

Apollo whispered to Venus, "Well, I soon will be Dad Owl again and you will be Mom Owl. Excited?"

Mom Owl nodded.

Mom and Dad Owl constantly checked on the two eggs in their nest, as well as the size and strength of the nest because this year's nest was very small.

Three weeks of time passed very quickly.

Tap, tap, tap were the sounds coming from an eggshell one morning. A baby's tooth had broken through the shell! With many wiggles, very slowly, the baby got out of the shell.

The baby owl, or owlet, could not see, but he had his mouth wide open. Mom Owl began dropping old worms into his

Hoo Hoo the Baby Owl

Written by
Duane Ziegler

Illustrations by
Katie LaFramboise

Hoo Hoo the Baby Owl
Written by Duane Ziegler

Illustrations by Katie LaFramboise

Edited by Kayla Henley

ISBN: 978-1-7377564-0-8

Library of Congress Control Number: 2021920584

Copyright © 2021 Duane Ziegler

Published by Duane Ziegler
Eagle, Colorado

All rights reserved. No part of this book may be reproduced by any mechanical, photographic, or electronic process, or in the form of a phonographic recording; nor may it be stored in a retrieval system, transmitted, or otherwise be copied for public or private use —other than for "fair use" as brief quotations embodied in articles and reviews— without prior written permission of the author/publisher.

Light of the Moon, Inc.
Book Design/Production/Consulting
Carbondale, Colorado
www.lightofthemooninc.com

This book is dedicated to
St. Mary's Catholic Preschool
in Eagle, Colorado

mouth. The owlet couldn't chew anything, just gulped his food down. The new baby was so hungry that Dad Owl had to leave the nest and search for more food.

Mom Owl spoke softly to her new baby, "Little puff ball, you sure are special. You have white and gray feathers sticking out all over the place."

The baby owl uttered, "Hoo, hoo."

Mom Owl worked extra hard on smoothing out the baby owl's eye feathers. "There," Mom Owl smiled. "You look so much better now." Mom Owl began to clean some soft materials away from the baby owl's eyes. Mom Owl said, "Yes, my little baby, soon you will be able to open your eyes and we will have fun feeding you."

The owlet replied, "Hoo, hoo," and opened his eyes and shouted loudly, "Hoo, hoo!"

Dad Owl returned with little frogs, reptiles, and mice for the new owlet.

Mom Owl announced to Dad Owl, "Our baby loves to say 'Hoo, hoo.'"

Dad Owl boasted, "Well, our Hoo Hoo baby is still hungry. We should call him Hoo Hoo. Mom Owl, it's now your turn to go out and search for more food. It is my turn to have some fun!"

Dad Owl whispered to Hoo Hoo, "Now you can see me. My name is Dad Owl and your mom is Mom Owl. We have many

things to teach you." Dad Owl was feeding Hoo Hoo at a very rapid pace. Dad Owl whispered, "Good boy!" Dad Owl explained how he belongs to the Ring of Owls. "We are a group of wise owls that help young owls learn how to survive in the sky, the woods, and help our friends whenever needed. A member of the Ring will visit us soon."

Hoo Hoo made a loud hiccup, as if to answer that he was full. Hoo Hoo closed his eyes and rested.

Mom Owl returned to the nest with more food for Hoo Hoo. Mom Owl commented, "This guy is always hungry."

Startled, Hoo Hoo woke up and opened his mouth again. After another feeding time, Hoo Hoo fell back asleep. The first wild day was over!

The next morning there was another *tap, tap* sound coming from the other egg. The shell opened up and another little owlet came into the world. Mom and Dad Owl immediately went to work caring for their new baby while also keeping track of Hoo Hoo.

The battle was on! Mom and Dad Owl caught mice, insects, and reptiles for their babies. The owlets didn't bite or chew anything, they just swallowed everything down, like they were never full!

The baby owls grew and grew. Mom and Dad named the newest owlet Hoots because he was hooting all the time. The owlets' eye feathers grew longer and made their faces stand out. They learned the importance of their clawed feet, called

talons. They also started hopping around on branches, being able to spread their wings.

One day, Hoo Hoo hollered, "Dad Owl, watch me hop and spread my wings. Watch me!"

They would try to play hide and seek games and tag. The most fun was when they would face their dad and sweep their neck in a certain way, turning their head almost all the way around, making click, click, click sounds and then laughing with Dad Owl.

Unlike his brother, Hoots chirped soft *hoo, hoos* with a hoot at the end, *hoo, hoo, hoot*! Soon, it became a common sound of the owlets. When the brothers were hungry, they would sing the Hoo Hoo song until fed.

As they grew bigger, the nest became smaller. The brothers tried balancing on tree branches, gripping with their talons, swaying forward and backward.

Dad Owl watched them closely. Dad Owl announced, "Tomorrow I will teach you to let go and land on the ground. You will need to work your wings to fly and get back up here in the trees. Then as a reward we will fly around the trees in our part of the forest. You will tip your wings to change direction. Then we shall practice getting into the air and good landings. I am excited to teach you!"

Sunrise came early the next day, and Mom and Dad Owl started lessons. Dad Owl demonstrated hopping from branch to branch and going through wing balancing techniques.

Watch me!

Then he had the brothers do the steps. They made very good progress. Dropping to the ground, the owlets gained experience landing, taking off up into the air and whipping their wings to gain height in the air. The brothers were having fun!

Mom Owl said sternly, "Now it is time for you to find your own food. It is important to be still and watch the ground with searching eyes. You need to be ready to jump quickly." Mom Owl described how animals travel, always looking for animal movements.

Dad Owl dropped to the ground beside Mom Owl and said, "Okay, no easy breakfast today. You must go out and find your own food!"

The brothers took the challenge and dropped to the ground,

hungry! Soon, Hoots caught a mouse. Hoo Hoo snagged a snake and fresh worms. Hoots and Hoo Hoo caught many insects. Mom and Dad Owl were very proud!

That night was story time again for the little owlets, now getting bigger every day. Dad Owl told stories of other owls in the forest, especially the famous ones. The famous owls were smart, courageous and honest.

The day arrived when two members of the Ring of Owls named Orion, named for the hunter constellation, and Titus, meaning the great defender, visited their home. Orion and Titus were checking on every home and welcoming new owlets.

Apollo greeted them. "This is Venus, and our little guys are Hoo Hoo and Hoots."

After being introduced to the owlets, Orion explained to them, "The purpose of the Ring is to help little owlets learn all necessary things to do in the woods, the sky, and especially how to obtain food. Some members of the Ring will help you learn as much knowledge as you can before you go out on your own to live. We will test you in making good decisions with your new knowledge. We assist and help each owlet choose their Owl name carefully."

Titus commented to the parents, "It seems your nest is too small to raise two owlets. Because of the small nest, we ask you to consider allowing Hoots to come live with me and my partner, Athena. We did not have owlets this year and we would love to raise your little one. It would help you and we would be happier also. We would visit on a regular basis."

Mom and Dad Owl discussed the offer. Dad Owl said, "That idea is a good one, but the boys will need to visit one another on a regular basis and come back home every now and then."

Hoo Hoo and Hoots touched wings, rotated their necks around and snapped them back and did another wing tap. Mom Owl tapped Hoo Hoo on his head a couple times and turned back towards the nest. It was a quiet time as Hoots flew away with Orion and Titus.

"Hoo Hoo," Dad Owl said, "Tomorrow after you get breakfast, meet me on the highest tree near our home."

The next morning, Hoo Hoo was up very early and met his dad high in the tree.

"Hoo Hoo," Dad Owl instructed, "Once we have taught you the necessary things you should know during daylight, then we do everything at night. Sleep may be a problem, but that is easy to fix." Dad Owl hopped up to the tallest tree branch and spoke, "Look over the forest for territory markers, like meadows, a stream, very big trees. At night we will notice the stars in the sky. Today we practice flying skills. We will fly together, making huge sweeps over the trees, diving and climbing in the sky. When we find a clearing down below, we will circle above it and dive to the ground, touching it as if you were grabbing a rabbit. Then you will grab air, whip your wings, going up as fast as you can. Ready?"

Hoo Hoo cried, "Ready!"

The owls began the flying drills. When they returned to the tall tree, Dad Owl approved, "Okay, it is your turn to fly alone around the forest."

Hoo Hoo asked, "Do you know when Hoots is coming back? I sure miss him."

Dad Owl replied, "Surprise me by bringing back something to eat!"

Hoo Hoo obeyed and flew into the forest. While looking for a mouse, he thought he saw Hoots. Before he could call out though, he saw a mouse scurrying and quickly caught it. Hoo Hoo came back with the mouse, but with the mouse in his mouth, he couldn't tell Dad Owl what he had seen in the forest.

Dad Owl said excitedly, "Good job, Hoo Hoo. Let's get some needed rest and then meet back here so we can do some night flying." Dad Owl flew down to a lower branch and went out of sight.

Hoo Hoo thought to himself, *I'm sure that it was Hoots down below in the forest. I am pretty lonesome. Who knows when Mom and Dad want to visit the Ring of Owls. Humph! Well, I am very lonely and this is my chance to be a grownup and see Hoots! Am I brave enough?* So away Hoo Hoo flew in search of Hoots. He had seen four owls together, so Hoots had to be one of them.

Hoo Hoo flew back over the area he had seen Hoots. No sign of him. Hoo Hoo searched and searched. Hoo Hoo searched

high and low around trees, in an X pattern, then a Z pattern. Still no sign of Hoots. He searched just above the trees, then down low around trees and bushes. Where was Hoots? Where did he go? What Hoo Hoo did find was a large tree with two large eyes and a nose just like an owl. He had found the Owl Tree! The tree was a little scary but also impressive! With the sky getting darker and darker, Hoo Hoo decided to rest and sleep. He thought, *I better get up very, very early, catch some breakfast and meet Dad Owl up on that tall tree.*

. . .

When Dad Owl reached the tall tree later that evening and didn't find Hoo Hoo, he flew all over the area, calling Hoo Hoo's name. There was no answer! Dad Owl flew back to the nest and asked Mom Owl if Hoo Hoo had come to the nest. Mom Owl hadn't seen him. Was he lost? They spent the whole evening looking for him. Both Mom and Dad Owl did not sleep that night. Where was Hoo Hoo?

The next day, Mom and Dad Owl were up early, but did not have breakfast. They flew directly to the tall owl tree. There was Hoo Hoo waiting for them. His mouth was full with two mice, a lizard, and his talons clutching a rabbit.

Mom Owl shouted, "Hoo Hoo, don't scare us like that!"

"I am disappointed you took off without telling us, but also proud you caught your mouse," Dad Owl admonished.

Hoo Hoo whispered softly, "I saw Hoots in the forest when I first caught the mouse. But I could not find him when I went back. I was just so excited to see him."

"We didn't know you were that lonely," Dad Owl said. "Let's go tomorrow to see the Ring of Owls and Hoots."

"Yeah, yeah, yeah!" cheered Hoo Hoo.

The next day was exciting because both Mom and Dad Owl took Hoo Hoo to the Ring of Owls meeting. Hoots was there and everyone was happy doing wing taps. Lots of wing taps! Hoots looked just fine. The brothers were laughing and soon a familiar song could be heard: "Hoo, hoo, hoo, hoo, hoot!" After much laughing and visiting, Mom and Dad Owl left to go home.

What a week it was for Hoots and Hoo Hoo! There were three other owlets and it made for wild competition. Besides Orion, Titus, and Apollo, other Ring of Owl teachers were Silas, teacher of the forest, and Felix, keeper of good luck. The instructors directed the air races where all five owlets lined up and flew to a designated area. There were Z patterns for all owlets to fly. Then, some instructors would fly directly at the young owlets, pretending they were attacking hawks. There were scary moments when the owlets would fly directly at a tree and then the instructor would holler right or left. There were situations where trees were marked and the owlet had

to swerve left, right, then up and down. They practiced wing tip control with more testing. The diving challenge was to dive at full speed and grab a ribbon with a soft landing. There were special practices for hearing skills and how turning the head increased hearing power. There were lessons for night flying and night hunting for food, and educational classes about wise owls and what young owls had to do to earn a name as an owl. Break time was very popular because of the large amount of food. The owlets would play tag and team relay racing.

"Tomorrow," Orion said, "We will have name discovery and review how you will get your new name. Now let's get some sleep and rest. Tomorrow is the big day."

Hoo Hoo was the earliest owlet to arrive in camp. Silas and Titus were in charge of the food. Hoo Hoo was first in line at the food table. While the owlets chowed down, Apollo, Felix, Titus and Orion flew by.

"Finish up your snack. We are to meet at the Owl Tree," Silas said

Hoo Hoo thought to himself, *I have been there before,* and said to the other owlets, "I am ready, follow me."

The owlets found the Ring of Owls sitting under the Owl Tree. The owlets took places in a semi-circle a few feet away from the Owl Tree. There were four male owlets and one female owlet.

Silas and Felix described the possible female names the female owlet could choose from: Iris, meaning the rainbow goddess; Minerva, the goddess of wisdom; Aurora, representative of the Northern Lights; and Hera, the goddess of marriage.

When they asked the owlet which name she desired, she answered, "Iris, after the rainbow goddess."

The Ring of Owls showed their approval by singing "Noc, noc, noc, noc, hoot, hoot, hoot, hoot."

Orion, Titus, and Apollo stepped forward. Titus described the names for consideration for the male owlets: There was Polaris, meaning the north star; Erroll, meaning an army commander; Argus, meaning seer of all things; Lucien, meaning to give light; Pax, meaning one of peace; and Regis, meaning a ruler.

Hoots immediately stepped forward and stated, "I would like the name of Regis."

The next names chosen were Polaris and Lucien. Then it was Hoo Hoo's turn. Hoo Hoo stated, "I want to be Argus the Owl, and I would be honored to assist the Ring of Owls in any work projects they may be involved in."

The Ring of Owls cheered the new owlets and their new names with their song "Noc, noc, noc, noc, hoot, hoot, hoot hoot!"

Noc, noc, noc, noc, hoot, hoot, hoot, hoot!

THE END

ABOUT THE ARTIST: KATIE LAFRAMBOISE

From an early age Katie has always enjoyed art and has been very creative. She has dabbled in all kinds of art from water colors, to acrylic paints, but her favorite is sketching, especially horses. She has a love for animals, so much so that she received a degree in Animal Science from Colorado State University in 2017. For the past couple years, she has enjoyed working as a Veterinary Technician and is very passionate about helping animals.

Illustrating children's books is recently a new endeavor. Katie loves helping the author's characters take form and come to life.

ABOUT THE AUTHOR: DUANE ZIEGLER

Duane Ziegler was raised on a farm in North Dakota with five brothers. While he had a strong attraction to the wheat fields, pasture land, and rolling prairies, the mountains of Colorado have been the biggest influence in his life. He has been a professional educator for twenty years and a professional real estate agent for twenty-three years. He is a member of SCBWI, Colorado Authors League, and Roaring Fork Writers' Group. His immediate family includes his wife, Sandy, two children DeAnn and Nathan, four grandchildren, and one great-grandchild. He thanks the many people supporting him in creating children's fiction.

Visit Duane's Website
duaneziegler.com

Or connect with him on Facebook
@duanezieglerauthor

**If you enjoyed this book, please visit duaneziegler.com
to learn about our other fun and educational books.**

OTHER BOOKS BY DUANE ZIEGLER

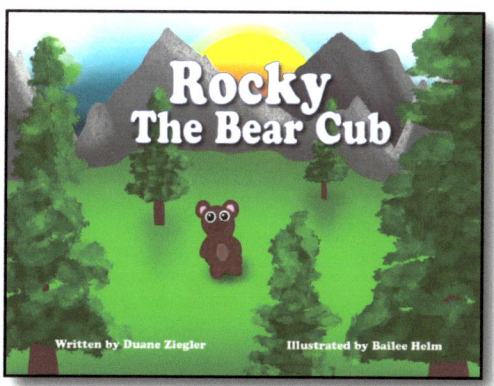

Rocky the Bear Cub follows a young bear cub named Rocky on his journey to say goodbye to all his forest friends before his first winter hibernation. Unfortunately, Rocky gets lost along the way while escaping a hungry coyote! It will take all his courage and the help of some new and unexpected friends to find his way back home in time for hibernation.

Goofus Galoofus is a young frog who dreams of being a cowboy and winning the Bullfrog Rodeo. Determined to prove his worth, Goofus disguises himself as a bullfrog and enters the Bullfrog Rodeo. But will his small size be able to match the other bullfrogs? And can he keep his true identity a secret?

Big Bad Brad is a small hummingbird with a big attitude! When Brad travels to the Rocky Mountains of Colorado to make a home for himself, his territorial attitude makes many enemies along the way, until some special friends teach Brad the importance of kindness and the value of friendship.

Visit our website for new books, coloring books, and to meet the characters!

duaneziegler.com

CHECK OUT THE JIMJIM SERIES!

The First Book In The JimJim Series

JimJim and his mouse family live near Sylvan Lake, high in the Rocky Mountains. JimJim and his brother and sisters must overcome the dangers of rainstorms, being lost, escaping Mr. Owl, dodging Rusty the Hawk, and dealing with Mr. Black Bear. Throughout their adventures is the chance to achieve greatness as a mouse and claiming their second name. Follow JimJim and his three siblings on their journey to survive the wilderness with the help of their new friends.

The Second Book In The JimJim Series

JimJim and his mouse family live near Sylvan Lake, high in the Rocky Mountains. Trapped in a backpack, the mice find themselves in Las Vegas. They have exciting times, but get swept outside into the street by accident. The mice are attacked by alley cats, visit many places in Vegas, learn new dances, make new friends, and learn karate. Follow JimJim and JoeJoe as they survive Vegas and find a way to return to Sylvan Lake with the help of their new friends.

The Third Book In The JimJim Series

JimJim and his mouse family live near Sylvan Lake, high in the Rocky Mountains. After a harrowing trip to Las Vegas, JimJim and his brother JoeJoe have returned home with their new friends Dr. Bruce and his assistants Haley and Danielle. Together, JimJim, his siblings, and their friends travel around Sylvan Lake helping animals in need. Follow JimJim and company on their adventures as they help the animals of Sylvan Lake and make new friends like Toby the Turtle, Sleepy the Mouse, Noah the Bunny, and Happy the Fawn!

Visit our website for new books, coloring books, and to meet the characters!

duaneziegler.com

CHECK OUT THE SAMMY PUFFIN SERIES!

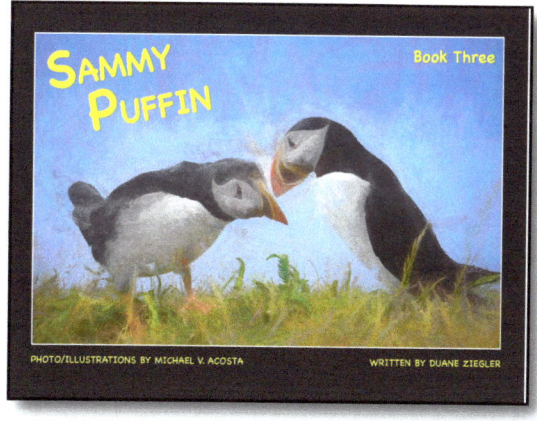

The First Book In The Sammy Puffin Series

Sammy Puffin and his puffin family live on the icy shores of Newfoundland where Sammy Puffin's parents teach him the ways of the puffin life: how to fly, catch fish, and spend time together. Follow Sammy as he has fun outings with Daddy Puffin and learns important lessons from Mommy Puffin.

The Second Book In The Sammy Puffin Series

Sammy Puffin and his puffin family live on the icy shores of Newfoundland. Now that Sammy has learned the ways of puffin life, it is time to put his lessons to use as he and his family encounter dangerous predators like Red Fox and Black Mink. Follow Sammy as he grows from a baby puffin to a young adult ready to venture off on his own.

The Third Book In The Sammy Puffin Series

Sammy Puffin and his puffin family live on the icy shores of Newfoundland. Now that Sammy is grown, he must leave the island with the other adolescent puffins to explore on his own before returning to start his own family. Along the way he meets Sarah and they become parents. Follow Sammy and Sarah as they have their wings full raising two boys, who seem to find trouble wherever they go.

Visit our website for new books, coloring books, and to meet the characters!

duaneziegler.com

www.ingramcontent.com/pod-product-compliance
Lightning Source LLC
LaVergne TN
LVHW071732060526
838200LV00031B/478